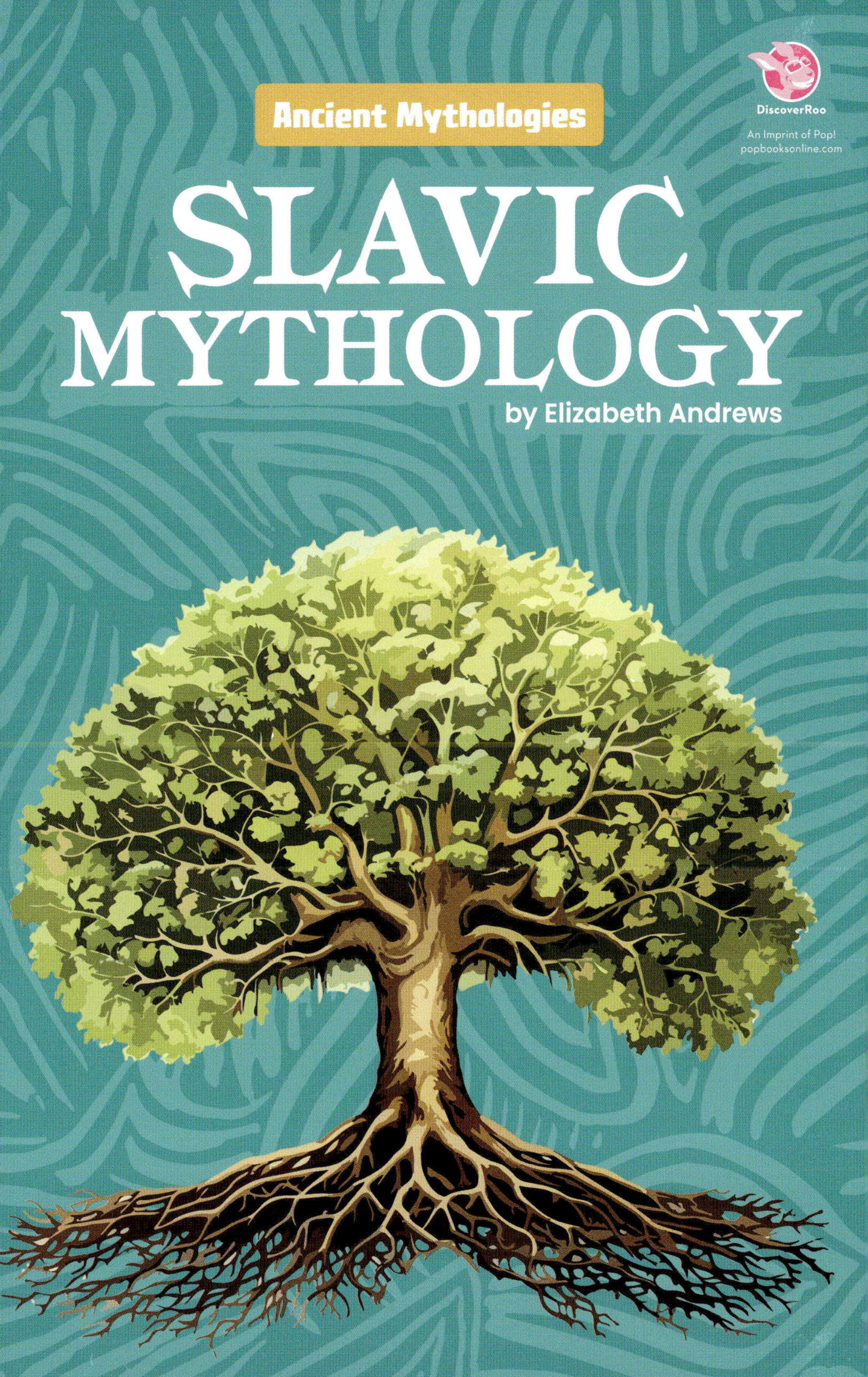
Ancient Mythologies
DiscoverRoo
An Imprint of Pop!
popbooksonline.com
SLAVIC
MYTHOLOGY
by Elizabeth Andrews

WELCOME TO DiscoverRoo!

This book is filled with videos, puzzles, games, and more! Scan the QR codes* while you read, or visit the website below to make this book pop.

popbooksonline.com/slavic-myth

abdobooks.com

Published by Pop!, a division of ABDO, PO Box 398166, Minneapolis, Minnesota 55439.

Printed in the United States of America, North Mankato, Minnesota.

102024
012025

Cover Photo: Getty Images

Interior Photos: Getty Images, Shutterstock Images, Alamy Stock Photo, Wikimedia Commons, Andrey Shishkin/Wikimedia Commons, Maxim Sukharev/Wikimedia Commons, Mhapon/Wikimedia Commons

Editor: Krissy Sterling

Series Designer: Colleen McLaren

Library of Congress Control Number: 2024938903

Publisher's Cataloging-in-Publication Data

Names: Andrews, Elizabeth, author.

Title: Slavic mythology / by Elizabeth Andrews

Description: Minneapolis, Minnesota : Pop!, 2025 | Series: Ancient mythologies | Includes online resources and index

Identifiers: ISBN 9781098247065 (lib. bdg.) | ISBN 9781098247621 (ebook)

Subjects: LCSH: Mythology--Juvenile literature. | Mythology, Slavic--Juvenile literature. | Gods, Slavic--Juvenile literature. | Deities--Juvenile literature. | Mythology, European--Juvenile literature.

Classification: DDC 299.18--dc23

*Scanning QR codes requires a web-enabled smart device with a QR code reader app and a camera.

TABLE OF CONTENTS

CHAPTER 1

COSMIC EGG

At the beginning of everything, there was only a dark sky and an old dark sea. Rod, a **divine** being, created a single **cosmic** egg from the darkness.

DID YOU KNOW?

Other societies also credit the creation of the world to a cosmic egg.

In the egg was the god, Svarog. His powers grew and cracked the egg. Svarog emerged and was cast in bright light. The dark god, Chernobog, came into existence in his shadow. Svarog glared at the dark sea and the god of water, Vodan, came to be.

The cosmic egg was made of gold.

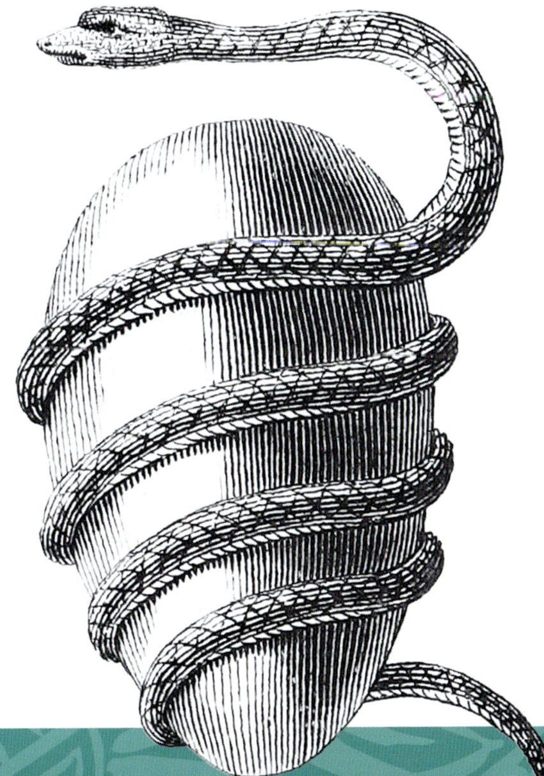

Some myths say Svarog had a beard made of fire.

The shell of the egg was very important. The top of the egg turned to dust and grew into the World Tree. The tree separated the earth from the **realm** of gods. In the roots of the tree was the underworld.

Svarog used gold powder from the underworld to create the world of the living, the sun, and the moon. After the world was made, Svarog used dust from the bottom of the egg to create humans. The gods watched over them.

Ancient Slavs gathered around oak trees for celebrations.

Myths are stories that often involve gods and **supernatural** events. They are not always based in fact. Myths helped people make sense of the world around them.

Slavic people have a four-faced god called the Worldseer.

Ancient Slavs lived in what is now known as Eastern Europe and Russia. Svarog and the egg is just one of many different stories of creation from the ancient Slavic people.

CHAPTER 2

SLAVIC GODS

There are many gods and goddesses in Slavic mythology. The most important and most **worshipped** are different depending on which region a person lived. Most often, Perun is considered the chief god of Slavic mythology.

LEARN MORE HERE!

Perun used lightning bolts as weapons.

The underworld Veles rules is described as a paradise.

Perun is the god of thunder and war. He is powerful and proud. Perun rules the skies, mountains, and godly **realm**. He carries a war hammer, an ax, and a bow that shoots lightning. His **nemesis** is Veles.

Veles rules the underworld, lowlands, and rivers. He is a trickster. Veles is a shape-shifter, but most often takes the form of a giant snakelike dragon. Even though Veles rules the underworld, he is not an evil god. He supports farmers. He also guides souls to their final resting place.

Svarog, the being born from the **cosmic** egg, is the god of fire and **blacksmithing**. He is very important to Slavic people. They live in an area where winters get cold and dark. Fire keeps them alive. Svarog is in a constant slumber. Some people believe that if he wakes, the world will end.

Dazbog gives gifts to people with good hearts.

Svarog has a son named Dazbog. He is the god of the sun and **prosperity**. Like his father, he is a savior during the winter. His spring sunshine brings rebirth in nature after the death of winter. Slavic people credit good harvests to Dazbog. They offer him **sacrifices**.

BLACK AND WHITE

The gods Belobog and Chernobog are opposites. Belobog is called the white god and Chernobog is called the black god. They represent good and evil. They are in a constant battle.

Today, Belobog and Chernobog are well-known Slavic gods. They were first mentioned by Christian scholars who visited the Slavic region in the 1200s CE.

Svarog's dreams create events on earth.

CHAPTER 3

THE IMPORTANCE OF TREES

Ancient Slavs **worshipped** trees. There were many deep, dark forests where Slavic people lived. The forests were scary but useful. Trees gave them furniture, shelter, transportation, and most importantly, fuel for fire.

EXPLORE LINKS HERE!

Some Slavic gods may live inside oak trees.

Horses and wolves often appear in Slavic myths. Wolves represent fearlessness. Horses are valued for their service to humans.

The World Tree is the center of Slavic beliefs. The World Tree contains three **realms**. The branches hold the realm of the gods. It is called Prawia. The trunk of the tree is the human realm. It is called Jawia. The roots of the tree are home to the underworld called Nawia.

DID YOU KNOW?

Oak trees are more likely to get struck by lightning than other trees.

Perun watches over Prawia. He appears as an eagle at the top of the World Tree. Veles lives in the underworld but travels between realms. He sleeps in his dragon form among the roots of the tree. Perun and Veles are always fighting each other. Their endless battles represent the natural fight for balance between **chaos** and order.

Chief gods in other ancient mythologies take on the form of an eagle as well.

Veles protects traveling musicians.

Veles enjoys his battle with Perun. Some stories say it began because Veles stole Perun's wife or cattle. Perun chases Veles between the realms. When they are in the human realm Veles turns into animals, trees, or other earthly things. Legends say that if lightning strikes a tree or rock, it means Veles is hiding there.

CHAPTER 4

MYTHICAL BEINGS

Prawia is home to more than just humans, animals, and plants. Spirits, monsters, and demons also live there. There are many stories of **supernatural** creatures connected to nature and its mystery in Slavic mythology.

COMPLETE AN ACTIVITY HERE!

A wolf used the water of death to bring a prince back to life.

Leshy may have been married to a creature of the swamp.

Leshy is the Old Man of the Forest. He is a guardian spirit. He exists in all Slavic forests. Leshy is usually heard instead of seen. People may hear his laugh and whistle. If someone does lay eyes on Leshy, he might appear as an old man who is missing eyebrows, eyelashes, and a right ear. Leshy chooses which animals hunters can kill.

DID YOU KNOW?

Sometimes Leshy disguises himself as a forest element, such as a mushroom, pebble, or animal.

Baba Yaga is a well-known Slavic myth. She might have begun as a gentle spirit like Mother Nature. Over time she became an evil witch who lives in the woods. Her home is a hut built on top of four chicken legs. Baba Yaga flies through the sky in a **mortar** steered by a **pestle**. When she passes overhead a storm follows.

Baba Yaga hunts, steals, and eats children. She looks for them while she flies. Sometime geese help her hunt.

Baba Yaga's house moves at her command.

The storms Baba Yaga creates are called tempests.

Baba Yaga represents the deadly winter storms ancient Slavic people feared. There are many stories about children wandering into the woods, never to return. Her story taught children not to go into the forest alone.

Today, Slavic people burn replicas of the goddess of death Marena to celebrate the end of winter.

Ancient Slavic myths have inspired many different stories and art over time. It is not the most well-documented mythology, but its existence helps explain what Slavic communities feared and hoped for long ago.

The Snow Maiden is a new Russian mythical character.

MAKING CONNECTIONS

TEXT-TO-SELF

If you were an ancient Slav, which god or goddess would you have worshipped? Please explain your answer.

TEXT-TO-TEXT

Have you read a book about a different ancient mythology? If so, what did those mythologies have in common with Slavic myths?

TEXT-TO-WORLD

With the help of an adult, research photos of Slavic forests online. Write a sentence or two describing what you see. Then, write about how you would feel living in a forest like that.

GLOSSARY

blacksmithing — the work of a person who builds or repairs things made of iron.

chaos — a state of utter confusion.

cosmic — relating to the wide universe.

divine — relating to gods and goddesses.

mortar and pestle — two tools used to prepare ingredients by crushing them.

nemesis — worst enemy.

prosperity — success or wealth.

realm — an area.

sacrifice — a person or animal killed as an offering to please a god.

supernatural — having to do with forces beyond what is natural.

worship — love, respect, and affection shown to an object, person, or being.

INDEX

This book is filled with videos, puzzles, games, and more! Scan the QR codes* while you read, or visit the website below to make this book pop.

popbooksonline.com/slavic-myth

*Scanning QR codes requires a web-enabled smart device with a QR code reader app and a camera.